HOW KATE WARNE
SAVED PRESIDENT LINCOLN

A Story about the Nation's First Woman Detective

Elizabeth Van Steenwyk

pictures by
Valentina Belloni

Albert Whitman & Company
Chicago, Illinois

For my KW friends who are so patient and wise—EAV

To my dear Mattia—VB

Library of Congress Cataloging-in-Publication
data is on file with the publisher.

Text copyright © 2016 by Elizabeth Van Steenwyk
Pictures copyright © 2016 by Albert Whitman & Company
Pictures by Valentina Belloni
Published in 2016 by Albert Whitman & Company
ISBN 978-0-8075-4117-3

Printed in China
10 9 8 7 6 5 4 3 2 1 LP 24 23 22 21 20 19 18 17 16 15

Design by Jordan Kost

For more information about Albert Whitman & Company,
please visit our web site at www.albertwhitman.com.

One day in 1856 a young woman arrived at the Chicago office of Allan Pinkerton, founder of the world's first detective agency. The woman's name was Kate Warne. She told Pinkerton she was a widow looking for a job.

Pinkerton never thought to hire a woman for a detective's job, but he was curious. "What would you do in this line of work?" he asked her.

Kate explained that women were more skilled in obtaining secret information. Men liked to brag about their adventures and women encouraged them to talk by pretending to be impressed. Women, she said, could also worm out secrets in places where male detectives couldn't go.

Pinkerton hired her the next day and, just like that, Kate Warne became the first female detective in the nation.

She disguised herself in fancy gowns and turned up at society parties. Many of the women there were married to successful men in business and politics, and they were eager to talk about their husbands' careers, especially to Kate, who they thought was one of them. Sometimes she dressed as a fortune-teller or wore other disguises to parties. She collected useful information this way.

One of Kate's first big cases involved a man named Nathan Maroney, who was suspected of stealing money from the company where he worked. She assumed the name Madame Imbert to befriend his wife.

Kate knew that Mrs. Maroney would be more likely to tell her secrets to someone who had something to hide as well. So Kate pretended to have a secret—a husband in prison. Before long she convinced Mrs. Maroney to show her where the stolen money was hidden, and Nathan Maroney was arrested.

Pinkerton and his men received glowing praise from the Chicago newspapers for solving the case, but Kate was never mentioned. Only a few people knew a woman had saved the day.

But Kate Warne's most important role was yet to come.

Abraham Lincoln was elected president on November 6, 1860, but many people in the southern states were opposed to his intention to abolish slavery. By the time he and his family prepared to move from Springfield, Illinois, to Washington, DC, six states had seceded from the Union. There were rumors that some Southerners were preparing to stop Lincoln's inauguration.

Pinkerton heard the rumors too. While in Baltimore on business, he learned that a group calling themselves the Golden Circle was meeting to discuss a secret plan against Lincoln as he traveled to his inauguration. Lincoln's travel route from Illinois to Washington had been reported in all the national newspapers, so his schedule was known to friend and foe alike.

Pinkerton called Kate to Baltimore immediately. Posing as a wealthy woman from Alabama, she infiltrated the Golden Circle by wearing a rosette on her lapel. All members wore such a badge to signify membership.

Kate soon learned of a plot to attack Lincoln as he passed through the city.

"He'll never leave Baltimore alive" was being whispered on the city streets.

By now the president-elect's journey had reached New York City. Lincoln would visit only a few more cities before he reached Baltimore. Kate traveled to New York to meet with a close friend of Lincoln and warn him of the assassination plot, while Pinkerton met directly with the president. The detectives had a plan to keep Lincoln out of danger.

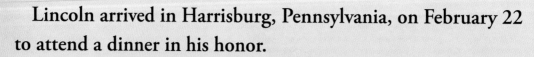

Lincoln arrived in Harrisburg, Pennsylvania, on February 22 to attend a dinner in his honor.

He was scheduled to take a train to Baltimore on his way to Washington the next morning. But instead, Lincoln would change his route and leave earlier than planned.

That evening, the Pinkerton Agency put the plan into action. Lincoln did not stay long at dinner. In his hotel room he disguised himself in an old shawl to cover his dark suit and a knit cap to replace his familiar top hat.

Then Lincoln and his companions left the hotel from a side entrance and took a short carriage ride to the Harrisburg railroad station.

A private train of only two cars was waiting to take Lincoln to an unscheduled stop in Philadelphia. As the train left the station, a Pinkerton agent climbed a telegraph pole along the route and sabotaged the wire so no one could alert secessionists down the line.

Kate and Pinkerton had already traveled to Philadelphia. Now Kate was waiting at the train station there. Her role was to save a place in the sleeper car for Lincoln and his companions on the train to Baltimore. Because the sleeper car had curtains, it was the only spot on the train where the president could ride without being seen.

But as Kate waited, the sleeper car began to fill with passengers. Thinking quickly, she told the conductor that her older brother was coming and that he needed privacy because he was ill and needed rest. The ploy worked. Nobody recognized the president-elect in his disguise as Kate led him aboard.

While he rode behind the curtains, Kate spent a sleepless night nearby.

Their train arrived at Baltimore's President Street Depot in the middle of the night. While Pinkerton stayed with Lincoln, Kate left the train. She would stay in Baltimore and listen for rumors of other plots to harm Lincoln. But she must have worried what would come next for the president—the most dangerous part of the journey.

The train had reached the end of the line in Baltimore. The railroad workers unhitched the sleeper car from the rest of the train, and a team of horses pulled it to a station across town to be hitched to another train. It was the only way passengers could continue a trip to Washington. For Lincoln, it meant he would be unprotected as the train car moved slowly through downtown Baltimore, a perfect opportunity for an attack.

But there were no attacks that night. No one knew Lincoln was on the train because he wasn't expected until the next day. At last the car was joined to the final train. Washington, DC, was only thirty-eight miles away.

The plan had worked!

The train arrived in Washington shortly after six o'clock on the morning of February 23. Two weeks later, on March 4, 1861, Abraham Lincoln was inaugurated the sixteenth president of the United States.

Allan Pinkerton hired other women detectives as a result of Kate's excellent work. When the Civil War began in April 1861, Kate often sent other detectives—men and women—to do dangerous work near or behind Confederate lines. She was so valuable to Pinkerton that he placed her in charge of his Washington office. She continued to work for him for several years.

When Kate died a few years after the war ended, she was buried in Pinkerton's private family plot in Chicago's Graceland Cemetery as a tribute to her service.

Her obituary was published nationwide and other women took note of her remarkable achievements. The suffragists Susan B. Anthony and Elizabeth Cady Stanton wrote about her in the *Revolution*, their newspaper about women's rights, noting her "good service for many years in watching, waylaying, exploring, and detecting."

"It has often been asked, would you make women police officers?" they wrote. "It has already been done."

And Kate Warne had done it well.

 NOTE

When Kate Warne stepped into Allan Pinkerton's office in 1856, she said she was a widow and that she had lived in New York before moving to Chicago. But little is known about her early life. She claimed no family and in some ways she was as much a mystery as some of the cases she worked on at the Pinkerton Detective Agency.

Like all women of that day, she had no citizenship of her own. Women weren't given the right to vote in the United States until the Nineteenth Amendment to the Constitution passed in 1920. At a time when women had few rights and received little credit for their work, Kate pushed boundaries and defied expectations.

The Pinkerton Detective Agency became the Union Intelligence Service during the Civil War, and its role in protecting President Lincoln made it the precursor to the U.S. Secret Service of today. After the Civil War ended, Kate continued to work for Pinkerton until her death in 1868, when she was just thirty-eight years old, presumably of pneumonia. At the time, such an early death was not unusual. Years later Allan Pinkerton mentioned Kate Warne frequently in his memoirs, bringing to light the important role she had served as the country's first woman detective.

Bibliography

Cuthbert, Norma B. *Lincoln and the Baltimore Plot 1861: From Pinkerton Records and Related Papers.* Los Angeles: Pacific Press, 1949.

Donald, David Herbert. *Lincoln.* New York: Simon and Schuster, 1995.

Pinkerton, Allan. *The Spy of the Rebellion.* New York: G.W. Carleton, 1886.

Stashower, Daniel. *The Hour of Peril.* New York: St. Martin's, 2013.